6085696000

BS

This book may be returned to any Wiltshire Library.
To renew this book, phone or visit our website:
www.wiltshire.gov.uk/libraries

Wiltshire Council

Also by Gethin Jones

Unconscious Incarceration:
How to break out, be free and
unlock your potential.

Available from Amazon

Edited by: Rebecca Thomas
thomasediting.co.uk

How to f**k up and still succeed

Use *Think it – Say it – Do it* and unlock your true potential

#TISIDI

Gethin Jones

Dedicated to
Hilary Stanton, Gary Clark,
Bruce Marr and Mark Legg

Contents

1: Rebirth

#TISIDI

You open your eyes and smile. It's an enormous smile. It represents the joy you feel in your heart. Your mind wanders back to the past few months and you say out loud, 'Yes, today is the day.'

Things have changed beyond belief and this thought fills you with immense hope. That fateful day when things changed was only two months ago. You remember your eyes opening and your heroin addiction taking hold yet again.

You remember the pain in your body. The prison of your mind just screamed and screamed. The only thing you could think about was how to get your next hit. You just wanted to die.

The memory of this makes your body shudder; you shake off the feeling like a dog shakes its wet coat. You swing your legs from under the duvet and, as your feet touch the floor, you feel your toes sink into the deep comforting pile of the carpet. You stand up tall, stretching as you feel the warmth of the sun through the curtains.

Pulling those curtains open, you're met by the brightness of the summer sun. The colours dancing before your eyes take your breath away. You are alive and free from addiction – the opportunities before you are limitless.

You last had this joy in your heart and mind when you were a child, with an innocence that allowed you to see the beauty of the world before you. Why, at 35, are you feeling this innocence again? Why this overwhelming sense that your life is just about to start?

You look in the mirror and see the colour in your face. No longer that damp pasty look that met your gaze for all those years. Your face is glowing with a light tan from the sun. Your eyes are sparkling – you can see them dancing like stars on the clearest of nights.

Your mind goes back to six weeks ago, when you walked into this detox.

—————••●●••—————

You are met by staff who have known you for years. You can see in their eyes that they want you to succeed this time.

You've been here so often before. So many times you have tried to fight the addiction driving you to a life of pain and destruction. The agony of your addiction creates the dullest of eyes; there's no sparkle there, just a dimming of a light before it dies. You're hunched over; weak, with no fight in you. Your body has been physically beaten and tortured by needles puncturing your skin. You haven't eaten a proper meal in months.

But deep inside you can feel a resolve, a determination that is building momentum. 'No more of this. This is my moment and I am taking it. Nothing is going to get in the way of me succeeding.'

There's a voice. It's Hilary – a true angel with a smile that warms the coldest of hearts. She's seen you come in and out of this detox for nine years. Hilary leads you to the medical room to take your blood pressure and prepares your meds.

'So, what is different this time?' she asks.

You try to find an answer but realise no words can explain the shift, the changes going on with your heart and mind. You look up and meet Hillary's smile with one of your own, fed by your deep resolve.

'I can't explain but I know that everything is going to change.'

Hilary leans over and gives you a hug. 'I believe you.'

The softness of her words and the warmth of the hug bring tears to your eyes. You have an ocean of tears inside that need to be shed. The pain you have held for so many years is ready to go now, so that you can live the life you always wanted to lead.

'Gethin, are you ready?'

The staff are calling. It's nearly time to go. Justin will be here soon to take you home.

As you walk downstairs, you see a new face; someone else is coming into the detox. You see yourself in them and feel so grateful that you made it through to this day. You see the fear and uncertainty in the man's eyes as he gets closer. You understand that fear and your heart reaches out to him; you want him to get to where you are now. You reach out and put a hand on his shoulder. You feel the shoulder bones protruding – no fat or muscle after many years of drug abuse.

His eyes meet yours.

'You will be ok. The staff will take great care of you,' you say and there's a look of hope in his eyes when he smiles back.

'Gethin. Are you ready?'

You hurry into the office, where you are met by the smiles of the staff. They radiate pride. You feel their belief in you. This belief is the fuel that has built the fire that is driving your desire to succeed.

Looking around the room, you are overwhelmed by gratitude for these amazing people. Your thoughts wander back to those early days again.

———————••●●•——————

You are withdrawing.

The physical aches are unbearable. Your stomach cramps and it feels like someone twisting your insides.

There's an aching deep inside your legs you cannot reach. No matter what position you put them in, there is no let up, no relief. Your whole body is screaming.

And your mind tries to manipulate you.

'You will fail. You will leave to get your hit of heroin. Imagine the peace and relief that would come with that one last hit,' it whispers.

Tears run down your face as you are physically and mentally tortured.

Then out of the darkness they appear. These wonderful human beings who are willing you on, telling you that you can do this. They are holding you with human love, care and compassion. Willing you to keep going as they see the potential you hold and the bright future that lies ahead.

––––––••●●••––––––

You leave the thought behind as you feel a tear running down your cheek. This is not a tear of sadness; it is a tear of gratitude. The people before you have done so much.

They have opened up your heart to all that is good in the world. As you say goodbye you embrace each and every one, thanking them for what they have helped you do.

Sadness and joy are mixed; you know it is time to say goodbye and step out into the world to start a brand-new life, filled with opportunity.

How To F**k Up and Still Succeed

2: What does a f**k up look like?

#TISIDI

That day in June 2006 seems so far away now. Little did I know then how much my life was going to change. My world today is so far away from where I once was. When I sit back and reflect, it's like I'm looking at someone else's life. I feel I have lived two lives in one.

This book is called *How to F**k Up and Still Succeed* and I believe we have all f**ked up at some point. Maybe some of you are still in that place now.

This book is an opportunity for you to start a journey using a model that will bring success. This can be personal, professional or within business.

This model works. How do I know? Well, that's easy. I just look around me now. I'm currently sat in my home, which has every comfort I need. I look out the window into my garden and can see the flowers begin to bloom on this beautiful spring day. I have a thriving business and so many people in my life who I love and who care for me.

This is a far cry from where I once was. If you read my first book, *Unconscious Incarceration*, you will know the pain of the life I once led. This book is the sequel but it still works even if you haven't read the first one (though I suggest you do). This book will help you learn about behaviours that get in the way of you becoming the very best version of you.

So, what does a f**k up look like for you?

Are you one of those people who go from one failed relationship to another? Are you the person who can't hold down a job or get promoted to the next level? Do you keep trying to set up a business and can't make it work? Or are you someone who is continuously fighting to lose weight, stop drinking or stay off drugs?

If you recognise yourself in any of these situations, this book is definitely for you. I want to share with you what my life looked like before I changed. This will put into context just how powerful my model is and how it can help you.

If you want to change your life for the better, for whatever reason, first you have to accept that you have a problem. We hear this all the time about alcoholics but it is true for all of us. We all have things we need to change. Other people can see what our problems are, in the same way we can see theirs. The gift of freedom comes when you can identify what you need to change about yourself.

Family history

I came from a dysfunctional, messed-up family. Social workers were there from the day I was born. My mum tried her best and I love her dearly. She had come through the care system and had a life that was filled with personal trauma. My father was an alcoholic and left when I was three year's old. This was also the first time I went into foster care. I stayed for a period of time and then returned home.

When I was five, my mum was with a new man and pregnant with my sister. During the pregnancy, my mum's partner had a fatal accident while working on the motorways. This led to mum having a nervous breakdown and again I went into foster care. A short time later I was returned home.

Soon after I came home, my mum started to see another man. He was violent, a criminal, and made mine and my siblings' lives hell. This was when my behaviour started to deteriorate. I would not take notice of any adult; this included my mum and social workers. My mum stayed with her abusive partner for a few years until they finally split when he got a 3-year prison sentence.

My behaviour did not change; instead I became less and less interested in the world. People who remember me say I was always a likeable and cheeky young man. I was not internally bad, I was just lost and trying to make sense of my world. By the time I got to nine, I was asking social workers to put me into care. Nobody listened, but more importantly no one asked why I was being so reckless.

Between nine and 11, I was running away from home and started to shoplift. I had regular contact with the police. At 11, I got my first criminal conviction, which led to my first visit to court. This did not deter me. I was determined that I would be better off in care and that my behaviour would make people take notice and listen.

Eventually I got my wish and was given a full care order. My life tumbled down a black hole that I was going to keep falling through for many years to come. The care system was not what I thought it would be and I became even more lost. I didn't want to be there but I had nowhere else to go.

Teenage Blur

My teenage years are a blur. From the age of 12, I ran away from children's homes and slept rough on the streets. My behaviour got even worse; I was glue sniffing and experimenting with drink and drugs. In January 1985 I turned 14; the age (in those days) that you could get a custodial sentence. Two weeks after my 14th birthday I was sent to a detention centre. These were brutal places. Every day I witnessed intimidation, violence and bullying. As a 14-year-old child, I was massively affected. Something inside of me just broke.

After leaving the detention centre, I had an internal shift that created the pattern for my life to come. I told myself: 'I'm not going to play their game anymore,' and 'The only person I can depend on is me,' and 'I am never going to trust another living soul.'

This thinking pattern sent me on a 20-year-path of self-destruction that looked like this:

age 13 – expelled from school
age 14 – secure units
age 15 – secure units and a second custodial sentence
age 15 to 35 – eight years behind a prison door
age 21 to 35 – dependent heroin user
age 35 – 57 offences and 18 convictions, no qualifications and no work history.

I was a walking disaster. If I was reading this I would say, 'Now that is some f**k up.' I would also be asking, 'So, how did he go from that to where he is now?'

The next chapters are going to answer that question. I will show you what success looks like. I will show you that no matter what your life looks like now, it can and will get better. You are now ready to understand my model. I call it *Think it – Say it – Do it* (#TISIDI).

––––––––––––– ··•●•·· –––––––––––––

You remember walking into that volunteering interview like it was the biggest day of your life.

You want to work with young people. You've been thinking that for a while. Your head is so negative and tells you this is never going to happen. You so want to share it with your friends. You want them to say, 'Yes, that's a great idea.' But your head is so loud that every time you try to say it your mouth opens but no words come out.

Eventually you find the courage and share your thoughts with your friend JP. Straight away, he says, 'Wow! You would be amazing – you have so much to offer.'

A glow washes over you. You have the widest of grins as you start to believe in yourself. JP suggests you talk to another friend, Trevor, who may be able to help.

You have learnt that the process of change comes with action. Quickly, you go to Trevor's to share your thoughts. Trevor's friend is there too as you walk into the room. You know each other but you don't trust him completely. You can't put your finger on it; there's an uncomfortable churning in the pit of your stomach.

You ignore your feelings and burst like a balloon as you tell Trevor your idea. He meets your smile with his own and repeats JP's support. You hear the other person speak, the one you don't trust. 'I think it's too early for you.'

Inside you feel an anger brewing. It's like the lava in a volcano about to erupt. This person is the negativity that has been sitting in your head for a lifetime. He is a naysayer. For whatever reason he is putting his own insecurities onto you. Your inner resolve replies, 'I'll show you.'

Ignoring the naysayer, you ask Trevor how you can make this happen. Trevor gives you the number of someone who could maybe help you find volunteering work. You leave the flat, beaming: you know the next step of your journey is about to begin.

3: Mind your mind (*Think it*)

#TISIDI

There are three principles: *Think it – Say it – Do it*, or #TISIDI.

Though each sounds simple, they all have their own complexities. I will take you through them, one step at a time.

Changing our behaviour, or in my case identity, is no easy task. (If it were, you wouldn't be reading this book). People across the world go on huge journeys in search of ways to understand themselves and maintain a change. You will know people who are living examples of this. They have overcome huge obstacles and are living lives that inspire others on a daily basis. You can be this person too. You have the ability to be so much more.

At the start of my journey, I was a hopeless drug addict with no qualifications, no work history and a criminal record as long as my arm. For years I believed my life was worth no more than a prison cell, a bag of drugs and no real home.

I am not that person today. I am a business owner, inspirational speaker, trainer and coach. I am educated to degree level. I am a father, grandad, uncle, brother and partner. Today I am successful, personally and professionally.

A thought comes before you make any changes. Your

mind has a million thoughts a day. Those thoughts tell you all sorts – what you should or shouldn't do, what you can and can't do.

They tell you you're no good and then that you are great. And they will tell you what to think about other people. Though sometimes the thoughts get deafening and all consuming, within this crescendo of noise, you will have thoughts that have merit and can start the change process.

Negative voices

I had many thoughts that told me 'I need to change'. The first time I tried to change was in 1997, when I was 26. I heard the thought 'I need to change' and took action by booking myself into my local detox. I remember being in that detox and going through both physical and mental hell.

The voice in my head said, *'You can't do this. You are not ready. Your problem is not that bad.'*

I listened to the voice and fell at the first hurdle. I went back to what I knew; a drug habit and committing crime to support it.

I bet you remember times like this in your life. Think now about the times you tried to do something new. I bet that most of your failures were linked to your mind; your mind bringing you back to the life you were used to. Like me, you would have failed because you didn't know your mind was your biggest enemy at that time. The *Think it – Say it – Do it* model is the solution to your mind's negativity.

Tomorrow never comes

Let's use an example most people can relate to. How many of you have decided you want to get fit? It goes like this:

You think, 'I need to take better care of my health.'

You respond consciously. 'Yes, I'm going to do this!'

You then start looking at activities and new diets. Your thoughts then start to say, 'You don't have the time, it's too expensive.'

The battle is now on. Some people will fail at this point.

Those who make it through and keep going, plan their next steps:

They say, 'I now need to make time to exercise and create healthy meals.'

Again, the mind jumps in and starts to say, 'Life is too busy. I can't fit it in.'

It may also say, 'Let's do this later, once life is a little quieter.'

Many will listen to these thoughts and their journeys will come to an end. Tomorrow never comes.

There are those among you who will fight past these thoughts, with grit and determination:

You start the new routine.

You start exercising before work or maybe at the end of the day.

You spend more time cooking healthier meals.

As a result, you've got less time for relaxation. And, guess what, the mind turns up the volume again:

You go to bed at night, confident that you will be up early to exercise.

You are 100% convinced this will happen.

You then hear the alarm. The room is dark, there are no sounds outside. The rest of the world are still sleeping and you want to join them.

Your head starts saying, 'Go back to sleep, you can do your routine this evening.'

You listen and turn off the alarm. When you wake, you feel you've let yourself down but convince yourself you will still get this done.

While at work, your head starts again…

'You are so tired; you have worked so hard.'

'You won't have time for exercise and cooking.'

'There is a good movie on the TV.'

'Get a takeaway; you deserve it.'

'You need to call your friends and family.'

Finally, you give in and say, 'I'll give it a miss today and do it tomorrow.' Tomorrow never comes.

That pattern has happened to me many times and I bet it has happened to you too. So, what separates those who succeed from those who fail? Well, I will tell you that the ones who succeed are the ones that use the *Say it* section of the *Think it – Say it – Do it* model.

Thinking on its own is not enough for the majority of people. The majority of people are prisoners of their minds; they are driven by their thoughts every day. They are what is known in the spiritual teaching world as 'being unconscious'. Their lives are being driven by the mind. In his book *The Power of Now*, Eckhart Tolle talks about how to become conscious; how to become an observer of the mind rather than a prisoner of the mind. This powerful book is well worth a read.

──────────••●•••──────────

You had no idea where Trevor's advice would lead.

It is now two years later and you have been in paid work for a whole year. You remember back to when Trevor told you what to do. You put this into action and just a few weeks later you were on your way to an interview as a volunteer. You had a name and address and a tornado of nerves spinning in your stomach. The feeling was so strong you couldn't eat all day.

──────────••●•••──────────

As you walk into the building you look again at the name: Tony Weeks. It seems familiar but you don't know why.

You knock on the door and enter. In front of you is a well-dressed man who is both tall and large. He welcomes you in and offers you a seat. You sit down and take in the room.

Then Tony says, 'Do you remember me?' He looks so familiar but you just can't place him. 'Sorry, I don't.'

'I looked after you in secure units when you were a child.'

Your world collapses at that moment.

'That's me f***ed. He won't give me a job now,' you think. Out loud, you say, 'Yes, I remember you now.'

He surprises you with a smile. 'You look really well and it's lovely to see you. What's happened to you since we last met?'

One thought asks, 'What shall I tell him?'

Another thought answers, 'Tell him the truth.'

You tell him about the disaster-filled life you have led; the years in prison, the drug dependency, the whole sorry story.

Tony takes a deep breath. 'You're very lucky to still be in one piece … So, how would you like me to help?'

These words are like the lifesaving beam from a lighthouse. Despite everything this man knows about you, he is still willing to help. You tell him you want to find a purpose and you need an opportunity.

Tony stands and says, 'I am happy to help. We take youngsters from deprived backgrounds out on our yachts. We also have a workshop where we build boats and carry out maintenance. I would be happy for you to do some volunteering in the workshops to start with. How do you feel about that?'

You grin like the Cheshire cat.

Walking home, it's like you are floating. Your life is growing so fast. Only a few months ago you were going from one disaster to the next.

Now it's the opposite; it's like the Midas touch where everything you touch turns to gold. You reflect on why that is.

You learnt some valuable lessons in the detox. Number one was about support. Everyone needs a support network. No one can create success alone. And you learnt what it meant to trust people, which let you take action on their suggestions. You can feel and see the change that is happening.

'YES!' You punch the air.

————————••●●••————————

A few days later you turn up for your first morning of volunteering.

First you are introduced to Nick; quietly spoken, he's calm and confident. Nick tells you he is a skipper and runs the youth sailing trips.

'There's a yacht that needs collecting from the River Hamble and we are going to get it now,' he says.

You take to him immediately. You feel no judgement from him. You feel he is a man who takes you as he sees you.

You pull into the Hamble and make your way with Nick to a 27ft yacht and before you know it, you're sailing gently down the river. You feel a joy and peace that fills your whole being. The river is like a mill pond and the sunlight is skipping and bouncing off the water. Beautiful green fields roll down and meet the water's edge. You watch the birds as they swoop down and skim the water; at this moment you feel as free as they are.

'Come and take the helm,' says Nick.

As you take control of the yacht you feel a sense of responsibility; this man is showing you he trusts you.

'Have you ever sailed before?'

'Yes,' you say. 'I sailed down this river when I was in a local children's home.'

Nick smiles and directs the boat into the channel so you can make your way onto the Solent.

'I have a good feeling about you. Before you know it, you will be taking kids out on a boat like this.'

As his words reach you, the negative voice in your head starts saying, *'You won't be able to do that.'* You push that thought away and look at Nick and see a man who is now part of your support network. This man believes in you and you will learn all you can from him.

You come to the last channel buoy and the Solent opens up. The view is a reflection of your life. You are now ready to move onto the next stage

4: Trust in others (*Say it*)

#TISIDI

One of the ways to learn to become conscious is to use the *Say it* section of my model. This is a key component and I will help you truly understand what it means. Only then can you move on to *Do it* and start to see the success develop within your life.

————••●●••————

Before that day when everything changed, you are wandering aimlessly. Every day is the same.

You wake with that familiar feeling of dread, which sits deep in your tummy, like a black hole sucking you in. You know your life needs to change. You can't keep living like this. You feel trapped and hopeless and there is no end in sight. Every day you go through the motions. You look at everyone else's lives and wonder why they have it and you don't.

'It doesn't need to be this way,' says a faint voice in your mind.

You know this is true but you can't work out how to change who you are. You stare at the wall, desperate for the solution. It does not come. You crumple into a ball just wanting something. Anything would be better than this. You just want things to be better.

————••●●••————

This is what life was like for me at the end of my heroin addiction.

I bet you've had these moments in your life too. Like me, you tried so many times to change. I heard that faint voice and sometimes I had the will to try and stop. Every time I failed.

I now know what I was missing. It was the *Say it*. I did *Say it* to many people – I was always saying 'I'm going to change' to my peers and the professionals around me. But I was not using *Say it* in the right way. There are a few things that I was doing wrong.

Take a moment and remember a time in your life when you wanted to do something different. You went to tell someone you knew and they came back with negativity.

'You can't do that.'

'It's too hard.'

'You can't afford it'

Yes, we all have them. The naysayers, the people who will never try anything new. They are usually stuck in their own lives and maybe don't have the confidence to do anything different. These people are dangerous when you want to do something new. You don't want to *Say it* to these people. I had this many times. I would tell other drug addicts that I wanted to change. They would say things like:

'It won't work, you are too addicted.'

'I have seen lots of people try – they all failed.'

'They will brainwash you.' (I laugh at this classic

response because, my god, my brain needed a wash!)

I don't want to be too harsh on these people because they are talking from their unconscious minds, which they truly believe. They are convinced that no one can change. They dismiss your plans because they don't want to see you succeed. Your success would challenge their beliefs and they are frightened of that.

Power of trust

Trust is the second element of when to *Say it*. Trust is hugely important if you want help to change.

Now remember times that you have asked for help (your *Say it* moments) and still nothing changed. Why didn't it work? Well, if you don't trust someone at a very deep level you will ignore what they say.

I had this with professionals. Though I would *Say It* to them, deep inside I didn't trust them. Professionals had been there my whole life and my life sucked. In my head, they were more of an enemy than a support. In my first book I talk about Jo. She was a professional who broke through my mistrust and connected to me as a human being.

Jo was the first professional I trusted and when I started to *Say it* to her, she advised me what to do and my change began. My keyworkers shook their heads in disbelief when I told them what Jo had said – they had been saying the same to me for years! They had, but because I didn't have trust, the advice could not sink in.

Can you think of a time when this happened to you?

You share a plan or an idea with someone in your family (you *Say it*). They give you some advice but it flies over your head – you don't get it. Then you share the same idea with another person, who you feel more comfortable talking to. They give you the same bit of advice but this time you understand it. You tell the first person, and they say, 'I told you that last week!'

Here is my example.

I am the owner of a limited company; my partner isn't. When I share ideas with her, I may not listen to her advice. Why? While I trust her to support me, I don't trust her business advice because she does not own a limited company like me. On the other hand, my friend Mark has been running businesses for over 10 years. When I share my thoughts with him, I will listen. Why? He owns a limited business and understands.

I'm smiling to myself here, as recently I shared some ideas with my partner and then Mark. They gave me the same advice but I disregarded what my partner had said. This led to a difficult conversation, as she felt I didn't trust her. I then explained that it's a different kind of trust. I explained there are parts of my life I trust her with that I wouldn't trust Mark with.

Your next step in the *Say it* model is to understand *what* you want to say.

What do you want to succeed in? Business? Relationships? Health and fitness? Or do you want to set yourself new challenges? Climb a mountain, learn to sail, become an actor, write a book? The possibilities for you are endless. The way they will come together is by saying this to the right people.

Asking for help

So what are we doing when we *Say it*?

We are asking for help. It is an acknowledgement that we don't have the answer. The day we truly ask for help, we show our humility by admitting that we don't know. This is when we can really use the *Say It* model to change. This is when we not only ask for help; we also accept the help that is offered. For the first time, your future is appearing on the horizon. You can see it.

Next you need to look at your circle. Does it include people who have experience in the area you want to change? Do you trust them enough to ask for help?

———••●••———

You are looking at your computer screen feeling very proud of yourself. You have just been given your start date to manage a young persons' service.

Your attention is drawn away by Bruce asking if you want a drink. 'Black coffee, please,' you reply. As Bruce walks away, you smile, thinking how much he has helped you. It's crazy, two years ago you didn't even know who he was.

As you look out of the window you reflect on the past three years and those who have supported your journey.

———••●••———

Nick was right, within a few months you were taking young people sailing. You continually challenged your thinking; every time your head said 'no', you countered it with a 'yes'.

When you asked what you needed to do to support the

youngsters on the boat, his simple reply was, 'Turn up early every day and book on courses.'

You have a deep sense of self-respect as you remember the effort you made and the action you took. You applied for a grant from the homeless charity Crisis. Your head was saying, *'You won't get that.'*

Again you ignored that voice and sought help from a lady called Emma Bushall. Not only did you get the grant, you also won an award from Crisis to celebrate your success.

You can see how all these people and all these steps have built your confidence. After a year of volunteering, you walk in and tell Tony, 'I think I'm ready to look for a paid job.' Tony says, 'Yes, you are and I am happy to supply a reference.'

That reference turns out to be gold and it doesn't take long for someone to see your potential. You are interviewed by Cecile and get a job at a local young person's hostel.

You remember asking Cecile for feedback on what was your first interview.

'You were just being you; don't ever stop being you,' she replies.

Just thinking of these words hits an emotional nerve. The words told you that *you* were worth something.

You remember getting that first payslip and the pride you felt. You were no longer dependent on benefits. This was huge; you had been on benefits for so long.

Cecile becomes a valuable teacher, as does your new supervisor Sandra. Together, Cecile and Sandra hold you, nurture you and challenge you.

Every day you turned up feeling that you did not belong; your head told you to leave. The thoughts were like torture and you knew why they were there; like it or not you were the least educated person in the room. This didn't mean you were unintelligent, it meant you had lots of new skills to learn.

You have been here a year now and it's your first appraisal.

You sit nervously with Sandra and say, 'I don't feel I am developing quick enough.' You're shocked by Sandra's response – a laugh. 'You have come so far in this last year. You've asked questions and I have suggested training or reading. You've done everything I've suggested.'

Sandra then starts to grin. 'What is that look for?' you ask. Becoming more serious, she says, 'I am leaving next month and I want you to apply for my team leader post.' Wow. You did not expect that. You take her advice and apply for the job. You prepare for your interview and go in remembering Cecile's words.

'Don't ever stop being you.'

You answer every question and leave knowing you could not have done any more. Within a few hours you are called into Cecile's office. You hold your breath and then hear 'Congratulations, you are my new team leader.'

It was amazing to see the pride in Cecile's face when she gives you the news. You look around the office and feel that you have arrived. You are no longer the least educated person in the room.

The team is looking at you to teach them.

———••●●••———

'Here you go mate.' It's Bruce, with your coffee.

You smile as you see Bruce has got black coffee too – you converted him from white a long while ago. He has become a good friend as well as a mentor. You laugh to yourself as you remember telling him, 'Bruce, you are my posh mate and I'm your bit of rough.' You have learnt so much from this man. Not just about work but also what it means to be a great human being.

You also remember how he's made you feel frustrated; the times you have looked to him for answers and his reply was always the same, 'So, what do *you* think you should do?'

Though frustrating at the time, you realise how he pushed you to learn more and start to realise your true potential.

'So, what do you plan to do in your first senior management position?'

You don't need to think about your answer.

'I am going to create a team that is both confident and competent. I am also going to study for my NVQ5 Leadership and Management qualification.'

Bruce smiles and puts out his hand, 'You will achieve both. I believe in you.'

These words have been with you from the first day in detox. You feel a warmth inside.

28

You are now able to put your arms around yourself and remember Hilary saying this exact same sentence to you. You remember Justin, JP, Trevor, Tony, Nick, Cecile and Sandra, who all believed in you too. The warmth inside is a new feeling.

A new door is opening. Today something has shifted and you finally think, '*I believe in me too.*'

How To F**k Up and Still Succeed

5: Change with action (*Do it*)

#TISIDI

The final section is simply *Do it*. Truth is, it's not that simple. You will know that the best things that you've achieved in life came through doing something (action). You may know the saying, 'If nothing changes, nothing changes.' How very true this is.

You may be one of those people who is always stuck in their thoughts. It's '*I'm going to do this; I'm going to do that*' but you never do anything.

You may even be one of those people who always say, 'I'm going to change this' or 'I'm going to change that.' You don't do anything and end up bored of the sound of your own voice. It's 'blah, blah, blah…'

I've been there. *Do it* is the step you need to take to fuel your success. I bet you know this. If you do, what stops you from taking action? In this chapter, I talk about two hurdles that I believe get in the way of most people's success.

Fear is the first and biggest hurdle. Fear is your greatest enemy. You can't see fear. It lives deep within your mind. It sits there quietly in the shadows, waiting. Fear wakes up when you have thoughts about doing something new. Then fear will start to tell you all the reasons why you shouldn't try to change.

You can learn to overcome fear.

Overcoming fear happens through self-awareness. Fear is what's called an 'interject', which is an influence or a rule about thinking that you've been given by someone else.

Interjects are often the voices that say, 'You should not do this ... you must not say this ... you cannot think this...'

When you were a child, you were most likely given interjects by your parents or adult carers and they probably believed they were doing the right thing by giving you rules about how to behave.

These interjects were given with the best intentions, but now they are a hindrance. These interjects create an internal narrative that is not yours. In reality, these interjects gave birth to the fear in your mind.

We are being influenced all the time by adverts, radio and TV. Eye-catching tabloid headlines are a classic! Today, I believe social media is the biggest culprit. It has the ability to create so much fear and invites us to make endless comparisons.

We compare ourselves to others, which then fuels fear and the insecurity that says *They are better than me. Everyone's better than me.*'

Investigate fear

Let's look further into fear. Earlier, I told you that fear is something you can't see. The fear lives in your mind and is created by the world you live in and fed by the information you are bombarded with every day.

Let's break down the word FEAR:

False
Evidence
Appearing
Real

It is the mind that makes it real. This false reality stops you from doing something new. Don't worry though; fear can be undone. Though there is a catch; fear can only be undone when we put in some action (when we *Do it*).

Let me tell you a short story that explains the process.

Johnny is a young boy in the playground at school. His best friend is talking about a monster under the bed, 'I can see the monster's shadows on my walls. I can hear the floor creak when it moves.'

'So, how do you sleep?' asks Johnny. 'Mum leaves the light on because the monster does not want to be seen,' his friend replies.

At tea time, Johnny's mum says, 'I've got a new film for you to watch.' Johnny sits down. The film starts; it's called Monsters Inc. Johnny watches monsters hiding under children's beds, trying hard not to be seen. After the film, mum takes Johnny up to bed. She gives him a big kiss and cuddle and starts to leave the room. As she does, Johnny says, 'Mum, please can you leave the light on?' Mum is curious; Johnny has never needed the light on before. 'Why?'

'There's a monster under my bed!'

Mum gently tries to reassure Johnny, explaining monsters are not real. Johnny trusts his mum with all his heart but right now the fear is strong and he does not believe her.

Time passes and Johnny asks his best friend if he has seen his monster recently. His friend laughs and says, 'There is no such thing as monsters.'

This makes Johnny question his own beliefs. When he gets home, he tells his mum what his best friend said.

'Mum, I'm not sure if there *is* a monster under the bed. What do you think?'

Mum pulls a thinking face. 'Johnny my love, how would a monster fit under your bed? And, I don't know if there is such a thing as monsters but if there were, wouldn't they smell really bad?' Johnny smiles and nods.

Looking towards the stairs, mum makes a suggestion. 'Shall we both have a look under the bed?' Johnny nods and takes his mum's hand – and a deep breath. Together, they look under the bed and, in that moment, just like magic, the fear disappears.

The action of looking under the bed is the *Do it. Doing it* changed the word FEAR to:

Factual
Evidence (that is)
Actually
Real

So, that's dealt with fear.

Face failure

The second hurdle that stops you from *Doing it* is failure.

Do you fear failure? Don't worry; you are not alone. It is

a natural way of being. Without the right mindset, failure can feed a lack of confidence. This is what then feeds the fear, as fear tells you that you will fail. This way of thinking sends you round and round in circles. Let me tell you what I believe the true definition of failure is.

The true definition of failure is *not to try at all*.

The first time I heard this it made so much sense. Think about how many times you have not even bothered to try to do something new. It may be a hobby, fitness, a relationship, a job or business idea. The list goes on and on.

I have a friend called Mark Legg (author of *The Business Builder*). Mark has had huge success and also experienced many failures. Like many, he has learnt more from his failures than his successes.

Mark once shared this with me and today I want to share it with you.

FAIL actually means:

First
Attempt
In
Learning

This really resonated with me. When you try something new you learn one of two things; it either works or it doesn't. Both outcomes will then lead to the next action.

James Dyson – who invented the Dyson bagless vacuum cleaner – famously stated that he'd created 5,126 prototypes. Did he fail 5,126 times? Dyson's mindset saw it differently; he knew that every failure would eventually lead to his greatest success.

Walking through fear and changing your mindset is something you can do now. You can do this with a deep desire to change. Create a support network, ask for help and take action. Nothing more, nothing less. The number one person who gets in your way is *you*.

--••●•••--

You love being on aeroplanes and the feeling of take-off; the acceleration that pushes you back into your seat.

You notice the different expressions on people's faces. Like you, some seem to be enjoying the feeling. Others are either gripping the arm rest or a partner's hand. They are probably not enjoying the ride but know it's something they need to do. The front of the plane starts to rise as it lifts off. You smile and reflect how the speed of the take-off has been similar to the speed of your change.

It is 2014, nearly 8 years after you walked out of detox. Today, you look out of the plane window. (You love the window seat where you can see the changing views and clear blue skies.) The bright sun makes you squint. You see the beautiful patchwork green below. You look out at the horizon knowing there is no destination you cannot reach.

You remember how small your world once was. You think back to that stinking flat and your daily walk to the local chemist. You remember the pain of that life and feel sadness for that part of you; the part that was lost for so long.

You shake off the sadness; it's not a time to dwell – it's a time to celebrate! You think of all the places you have been. You sailed a yacht from Portsmouth to Lisbon, (now that was an experience). You have been to Corfu, Antalya and Oludeniz in Turkey, to Egypt's Sharm El Sheikh and Hurghada, Gran Canaria, Fuerteventura, Tenerife, Milan and sailed yachts around the Caribbean. You've even bungee jumped in Switzerland. You have done so much; the list goes on and on.

You start to think about the past two days and what could come from this journey. A pharmaceutical company had paid for you and your colleague Sue to fly to deliver a workshop in Birmingham and you are on the plane heading back home.

You've been flabbergasted by the whole experience, from booking into the Hilton Hotel where the conference was being held, to getting access to the VIP lounge on the top floor.

The building is huge. Everyone is well dressed and looks like they belong.

Even after all these years, you have a deep thought that sometimes says, *'You don't belong.'* You ignore it and smile to yourself. You know this thought sits within everyone. It's the imposter syndrome and the message it makes you hear, or feel, is 'somebody's going to find me out'.

You get to your room and you realise it is not a room, it's a suite! At the floor-to-ceiling corner window, you take in a panoramic view over a lake. You shake your head in disbelief as you hear a voice saying, *'You are so lucky.'* You look at yourself in the mirror and think, *'Luck has nothing to do with it, this comes from lots of hard work.'*

'Would you like a drink, sir?' It's a member of cabin

crew. 'Yes please; black coffee, no sugar.'

'Tea for me please,' says your colleague Sue (you haven't converted her to black coffee yet). 'What did you think of the event?' she asks. You give a wry smile. 'It was great, but I still can't believe we got all that and got paid for it too.'

Then you say, 'I still keep thinking about that after-dinner speaker.'

You look out of the window and think back to the dinner; around 300 people, all well fed and watered, sat waiting for the guest speaker.

——————•••● ●•••——————

'Ladies and gentlemen,' the compère declares. 'Please may I introduce tonight's speaker, who will be talking about his relationship with alcohol.'

As you watch the man walk to centre stage, you can feel his nerves. He is perspiring. He starts to speak. You know his story of a dysfunctional life; his pain connects with your own. You hear how he tried to numb his pain with alcohol but how this only brought more pain. It is obvious he is still hurting.

You then hear how he used sport to overcome his demons. You have more questions than answers: has he truly dealt with his trauma?

You hear how he spends a lot of time away from his family, training and racing. You wonder if he is using sport to cover the pain and if he is actually still hurting those he loves.

You clap along with everyone else. You have to take your hat off to the man. He has overcome so much; look at what he's doing today.

As you clap, you hear a voice inside. *'I could do that too.'*

Sue interrupts your thoughts, asking what you thought of him. 'He was ok,' you reply. 'Yes – but you could have done a better job'. You laugh and whisper, 'I thought the same thing.'

--------••●••--------

The seat belt sign comes on. Everything is getting closer, the cars on the roads, the houses and what's in the gardens. Your view is changing.

You realise your horizon is going to change again too. You've thought non-stop about one thing. Just before touchdown you lean over to Sue, 'You're right, I *am* going to become a public speaker.'

'Fantastic,' she says. 'You will be wonderful.'

How To F**k Up and Still Succeed

6: Learning to drive

#TISIDI

You now have the outline of the *Think it — Say it — Do it* model. This isn't enough on its own. You need more information. Imagine I have just given you the keys to the *Think it — Say it — Do it* car. It's amazing. This car can take you anywhere you want to go. Next stop, change! But you don't know how to drive it. You need some lessons.

Driving lesson number one; this is about creating the support network I mentioned in the last chapter. This is essential. No matter how confident you are, you will need help from others. A support network can shift and change depending on what you need help with. My first support network was my detox unit. In the unit I became surrounded by people who could help me change. It was a safe environment where I could learn to start sharing my ideas of what I wanted to do. This was my first step to change.

I would like to say that engaging with a support network is a simple thing to do. But, guess what, your mind usually has other plans. Remember, it doesn't like change!

Think about walking into a new room for the first time. All of the people in there know each other. You are the outsider looking in. Your head is telling you to leave, saying you don't belong there. You become self-conscious and self-obsession kicks in. This is the moment you have to dig deep and find that inner strength that will take you forward.

41

Let's also be honest; not everyone in this new network will have the experience or answers you need. You have to go through a process of trusting these new people in your network.

When you join a support network, lots of people will be offering you advice. You take them at face value. Why not – you don't know what they know. You are there because you admit that you don't know and need help or guidance.

Importance of trust

When you first join any group, you usually know you are the least intelligent person in the room. This doesn't mean you are stupid; it means you are about to learn something new. I remember this in the detox. I saw a mixture of people and they all had lots of advice for me. I listened to what was being said. I wanted to change but I was not sure who I needed to listen to. More importantly, I wasn't sure who to trust.

Trusting someone new is not a simple thing to do. Think about your life now; how many people do you truly trust? How many times have you asked for help? You are stuck in a place where you no longer want to be. You are unhappy at work. You may be in an unhealthy relationship. You may be struggling to take that next step with your business. Or you may be feeling that your life is going nowhere. You have asked for help so many times, but nothing has changed.

This is because of your mind. In your head, you believe you know what it is you need. You have created a vision of what you believe the answer is. This means that when you are given a solution that does not meet your vision you disregard it. You disregard it because you don't trust them. This is why so many people get stuck at *Think it – Say it.*

What you need to learn is how to accept the help being offered.

Accepting the help is what so many people miss. They are usually saying '*no one ever helps me*'. The truth is they don't allow people to help. At this point you need to open your mind; say to yourself, '*Maybe they know better than me.*' You then have to take the advice given and move to action. You will then know if it worked or if it didn't. Either way, you have started to move away from the problem and into the solution.

Not everyone in a support network will be able to help you. The people you need are there, but you need to find them. The process of trust comes when we have a strong relationship. I believe trusting relationships follow a format:

rapport – early conversational exchanges, the getting-to-know-you process

test and deliver – you ask for advice or a suggestion

trust – the person consistently delivers and meets your needs.

The test and deliver stage is fundamental. It can be something simple, like asking a question about next steps, or asking to meet up on a 1-2-1. If the person delivers and it adds value, they become integral to your development. If the person you ask does not deliver, it's time to move onto the next person.

I call this creating a 'power of five' (I cover this in more detail in a later chapter). Look at your life and those around you. You represent the five people you hang around with. When I needed to stop taking drugs, I created a network of people who did not take drugs. When I wanted to get a job,

I created a network of people who all had jobs. When I wanted to become a business owner, I created a network of business owners. This is sometimes called *sticking with the winners.*

Networks change

Support networks come and go. I learnt that there comes a point when you can become the most intelligent person in the room. When this happens, it is time to move on as you are no longer learning. The *Think it – Say it – Do it* model is one that keeps you moving within your life. We are never the finished product. I am currently investigating my spiritual self. I am now joining new networks. In this area I am the least intelligent person in the room.

There is a final part in relation to your wider network. As your life develops you will naturally move from one group to another. This does not mean you have to leave everyone behind. Some people will stay with you always, no matter where you go. I once heard that people come into your life for either 'a season, a reason or a lifetime'. This is so true within support networks.

The 'seasons' are the people who give you a golden nugget and then just disappear.

The 'reasons' mentor you and become your teachers.

And finally, you have those people who cross over into friendships and last 'a lifetime'.

Seeing yourself in the rear-view mirror, you know you are looking the part.

You are about to go into your first Professional Speaking

Association (PSA) meeting. This is a network of professional speakers that gives support and training to those wanting to create a speaker business.

You feel so nervous. It's like your first day at school; new kid who knows no one. You've been in touch with a guy called Peter Green about this group. He was very engaging on the phone and his encouragement got you here.

You take a deep breath and think back to how you got to this point.

The thought of becoming a public speaker never left you, though you did nothing with it.

Life is funny sometimes and next steps come unexpectedly. You are in the office one day and a gentleman is introduced to you as a new starter. Your face lights up – you knew him during your early days of change.

You reminisce about your individual journeys. Paul is working here part time while he sets up a new business. Your ears prick up.

'I worked at IBM for years and had a really great job and good future,' he says. 'I knew how lucky I was, but I just had a thought that I wanted to do something different. I had an idea that I wanted to set up a coffee shop. I wanted it to be a social enterprise that supported people in early recovery.'

'Wow,' you say, 'This is great. How did you get it started?'

He tells you how he joined the School for Social Entrepreneurs and started to learn about how to become a business owner. You are gripped; what he is sharing is a gift from the gods. As he speaks, your mind is racing with thoughts about how you can set up a business too.

The next day you see another friend called Vince, who you've known for a while. He's a wise bloke, who leads the training department. You tell him about your idea to become a public speaker and he suggests you try using LinkedIn to build a network.

That night you walk home with a spring in your step. You can't wait to fire up the computer. You log onto LinkedIn and search for public speakers. You find a 'professional' speaker called Lee Jackson. You look at his profile and think he could be someone who could offer some good advice.

You find the courage to direct message Lee. (Your head says, *'He will not reply.'* You ignore it.) Next day you see a message notification on LinkedIn; you don't open it and go and make a coffee. You return to the computer and stare at the notification. Your head tells you all the reasons Lee will have given for why he can't help you. Finally, you open the message.

To your surprise, Lee gives you the option to call him later that day. You are excited and nervous. You overcome your fear and call Lee. You hear a strong Yorkshire accent and straight away he puts you at ease, asking, 'What it is you want to do?'

You tell him the story of your life. You share your trials and tribulations; the successes, the failures and the desire to set up something new. Finally, you tell Lee about the idea that was formed when you heard a speaker in Birmingham.

Lee listens without interruption and when you finish, he says, 'That is some story! Can I give you a small bit of advice before we start?'

'Of course,' you say (*any advice would be welcome.*)

'Don't call yourself a public speaker. Public speakers speak in church halls and people expect this for free. Call yourself a professional speaker; this means you expect to be paid as it is your profession. It took me a year to learn that,' he adds.

It makes so much sense. It is Lee who then puts you in touch with Peter Green, chair of the PSA.

–––––––––––––– ••●●•• ––––––––––––––

Your phone beeps. You are still looking in the mirror. It's now or never. You step out of the car and stride to the entrance.

Going through the door, your confident stance and smile disguise the nerves. There are about 30 people in the room, all dressed to impress. Flamboyant, you can see the performer within them all. You scan the room for Peter – you know his face from LinkedIn. Spotting him on the other side of the room, you walk across without thinking and introduce yourself.

He shakes your hand firmly. 'You made it – it's good to see you.' Peter starts to introduce you to other speakers. When they ask about your speaker business, you explain, sheepishly, that you haven't got one yet. They reassure you that you're in the right place and will learn a lot.

–––––––––––––– ••●●•• ––––––––––––––

Peter raises his voice. 'Ladies and gentlemen, please make your way through. We are about to start.'

Peter is heading for a stage. You see seats at the back and head for them but then you stop and look to the front. You see vacant seats there too. You tell yourself, *'I'm going to sit at the front. I'm here to learn as much as I can.'* Taking your front row seat, you see nods from those around you. You get out your pen and paper, and smile.

The smile is an acknowledgement of the courage it took to get here, and you know that a new journey is about to start.

7: Powers within

#TISIDI

Driving lesson two is about what keeps the car on the road. Cars need a mixture of ingredients to work; petrol or diesel, oil, brake fluid, engine coolant – even windshield wash is a must.

To be successful in the *Think it – Say it – Do it* model, you will need the right fuel to get you from initial thought to final outcome.

In this chapter I will explain the 'foundation principles', why you need them and how they work. These principles are:

self-belief

open-mindedness

honesty.

These are the behaviours you need to support *Think it – Say it – Do it.*

I have noticed that the most successful people in life have two things in common. (When I say successful, I mean people who go through life with a smile and achieve both personally and professionally.) My power of five people all have high levels of self-awareness and emotional intelligence.

Though I'm sure many of you understand the term 'self-awareness', maybe some of you are scratching your head at 'emotional intelligence'.

I was like this once. I had no idea what emotional intelligence was. If this is you, don't worry. Emotional intelligence comes naturally as you become more self-aware.

Self-belief

Self-belief is a key component; it's the fuel gauge you have to monitor every day. If you don't believe in yourself, how can you expect others to believe in you?

Some people seem to have a natural in-built self-belief. They are the types who are unshakeable and are not impacted by what the day brings. If this is you, then you are one of the lucky few. If this is not you, don't worry; self-belief can be developed.

You will know if you lack self-belief as you will rarely get out of the *Think it* stage. This is because your mind will pooh-pooh your thoughts by saying, *'You can't do that.'* Is this you? If it is then your first step is to go from *Think it* to *Say it*. You just need to *Say it* to the right person.

I had to develop self-belief as I had zero belief in myself. Today my self-belief is unshakeable and I know that there is nothing I can't achieve.

The people you share with at this stage are key.

The people you share with will be the ones who believe in you.

It's like a parent who holds a child. They believe in their

child. They will encourage them. They will nurture them. They will do this until the child stands tall and says, *I can do this'*.

If you have tried to create self-belief and failed, I have a tip for you. The tip will work but only if you *Do it*. Remember nothing will change without action.

Ok, so here it is.

Every morning for the next 30 days I want you to look in the mirror.

I want YOU to look at yourself. I want you to look deep into your eyes. Now tell yourself these three things:

I believe in you.

You can be anything you want to be.

Today I will... then set a goal linked to your long-term vision.

See how the belief in yourself changes over the 30 days.

This works because you are telling you. You are taking care of you. This is the long lasting sort of care; self-belief is like a plant that is growing within you. Your self-affirmation is the food that plant needs to grow.

Open-mindedness

How open-minded are you? I have heard people say they are open-minded but in truth they are not. These people rarely listen to anyone else. They believe they know best but really, they are closed-minded.

Being open-minded can also be called having a growth mindset and being closed-minded is having a fixed mindset. There's lots of literature available on mindsets and all evidence shows that the most successful people are open-minded and so have a growth mindset.

Let's look at this in relationships. How many relationships break down because a partner is not being heard. Every idea they have is dismissed. They are met with 'it's my way or the highway'. On the flip side, a relationship that has two people with open minds lasts. The relationship is equal and they both listen and learn from each other.

Business leaders and managers are the same. Yes, they are in charge and final decisions sit with them. This does not mean they have all of the answers. These leaders and managers are open to ideas and empower those around them. They don't see peers as competitors; they see them as people who can help them to grow and succeed.

You may believe you are open-minded. Is this the truth or an illusion? Only you will know. This is where self-awareness links with self-honesty. It is easy to be open and aware of all that is good about us; the real growth comes when we identify what is less good about us and is a barrier to our success.

Honesty

This takes us to honesty. I don't mean honesty in relation to stealing or manipulating people. I am talking about a self-honesty that sits within you.

I mentioned earlier that the only way to fix a problem is to identify there is one. You identify the problem by being honest with yourself. Self-honesty is how this happens.

In truth, others may tell you that you have a problem. Like most people, you will usually push this away. You do this because you are being told you are wrong. No one likes to be told they are wrong. Even when we are wrong, we will defend our wrongness. We will justify our actions because we don't want to admit we are at fault.

Self-honesty is not a weakness; it is a strength. It means you are open to understanding more about you. It's not easy to practise at first. The best way is to take some time to be quiet. Some call this being mindful, or meditation.

Look at your life. Look at what you have done or what you have not done. Identify the patterns of behaviour that are the issue. You can then take these to your support network (*Say it*), who can give you the solutions you are seeking.

------------••●●••------------

The room is far bigger than you thought. There are over 250 people and you are on stage next.

You are clear what you are going to talk about and share. And you wonder how you got to this point. While you were in the detox you met a group of people who shared a way of living. These people were content – you could see the light in their eyes. You could hear the success in their lives when they spoke. They didn't take drugs any longer and they had jobs, homes, families and good lives.

You remember listening to them sharing how they succeeded. They all had a self-belief that you could feel. The honesty they spoke about was something you had never heard before. They all talked about the journey of discovery that brought about high levels of self-awareness. You sat on the edge of your seat. You were hungry for change.

You put up your hand and ask nervously, 'What was the first step on your journey?'

A gentleman in his early 50s answers gently, 'That's easy, I had to open my mind. I was so closed-minded and believed I had all the answers. How many times have you been here?'

'Fourteen.' Your head is down, embarrassed.

The man smiles and explains that he too kept going round and round in circles.

His honesty makes you feel better. He is saying that he is not perfect. 'I had to change my mindset and thinking. Every time I went into group I would shut down. I told myself I knew it already.'

His next words are profound and life changing for you.

'I did know what was being said – I'd heard it all so many times before. We will all sometimes reply saying "I know, I know, I know" but knowing is not enough. The power comes when we put the knowing into action and then we start doing.'

Back in the hall it is nearly time. The compère is introducing you. Applause. You walk to the stage, heart pounding, mind trying to focus on the next 45 minutes.

Then silence. Deafening silence. You look out at all the faces looking at you. In a split second, you remember all you have been taught and you connect with your self-belief. You take a deep breath.

Your mind speaks to you, *'You have something to say and now's the time to say it.'*

You start to speak, knowing that not everyone in the room will connect with what you are saying. They may be closed-minded. Your mind is open. You know you can't change everyone's opinion.

You show your honesty and tell them who you truly are; the damage you caused yourself and others. You look out into the audience. They seem to be hanging off your every word. You show confidence and vulnerability.

As you speak, you hear Cecile's words. *'Don't ever stop being you.'*

This inner voice tells you that you are ok. You notice the speed you are talking at and that you are pacing from one side of the stage to the other. As you notice this, you remember being back at the PSA.

••●●••

You sit down with Peter, having just delivered a talk to your peers for the second time. His warm smile puts you at ease, as always. 'Ready for our feedback?'

'Yes.'

Your message is on point. The way you engage the audience is a pleasure to watch. You can see them living your experience. The main issue is your nerves.

Peter's words hit you hard. Your defences rise and you stay silent as he goes on.

'When you are nervous you speed up your delivery, which makes it hard to keep up and to feel what you are saying. And you start pacing from side to side. This is also distracting. It takes the audience member out of the moment you have put them in.'

He suggests you add pauses and use them to reflect on where you are standing and how fast you are speaking. You thank Peter for the feedback but inside you believe he is wrong – you'd got applause and slaps on the back!

Driving home, you reflect on your talk. You remember how much you were moving. You remember that the talk should have lasted 20 minutes but you finished it in 17. You smile and realise that Peter was right.

—————— ··•●•·· ——————

You hear yourself speaking as you reach the end of your sentence. You use this moment to take a breath. As you breath in, the audience relaxes.

Taking Peter's advice, you centre yourself on the stage. You start to speak at a slower pace. You see the audience lean forward, pay attention. You come to the end and thank them for listening. You are met with a huge round of applause and beaming faces.

As you leave the stage you say silently, '*I thought it, I said it, I did it.*'

8: The power of five

#TISIDI

So, what do I mean by the 'power of five'?

For me, this underpins the whole *Think it – Say it – Do it* model, so I will dedicate an entire chapter to it. What I know today is that you reflect the five people you spend the most time with.

We learn and develop through these people; they help us create our beliefs, values and opinions.

This happens from the day we are born – the first power of five is our immediate family. We learn from them and it is they who influence who we are and the beliefs we have about the world around us.

I once heard this saying:

'What we see we learn,
What we learn we practice,
What we practice we become,'

There is then a final line that can be true for some:

'What we become is not always who we are meant to be.'

This final part resonated with me and was one of the reasons I made the changes I made. I looked at who I was and started to question, 'Who am I really? What do I truly want to achieve?'

Positive and negative

Powers of five can be positive and negative and we have to acknowledge both. I will start with the negative. If you are around people who are always moaning and never see the good in anything then this will stunt your development. This kind of person will put others down. They will not be encouraging. They will look for every reason why it won't work. These people will see everything as a drama.

I grew up with negative powers of five. My first power of five was created in children's homes. We were all of the same ilk; we didn't trust the adults around us so we learnt from each other. Many of my peers smoked, so guess what? I learnt how to smoke. Many of my peers committed crimes. Guess what? I learnt how to commit crimes. Many of my peers used drugs to escape. Guess what? I learnt to take drugs!

My second power of five? I created that on the streets, in prisons and drug dens. My peers there told me I could not trust the system. Guess what, I didn't trust the system. They told me that people like us could never give up drugs. Guess what, I never tried to give up drugs. They told me that I would never get a job with my criminal record and, guess what, I never got a job.

Drains and radiators

In life we have two types of people. They are either drains or radiators.

Let me explain both to you now.

Drains are exactly that; they will drain all of your positive energy. They just take, take, take. They are a glass-half-empty and will always focus on the negative. They will always have a drama going on and if they haven't, they'll create one.

Radiators will radiate positive energy. These people are a glass-half-full. They will be naturally nurturing, encouraging and supportive. These people will listen to you, understand you and guide you in the right direction. They will see every situation in life as an opportunity to learn and develop.

Today I choose to be around radiators and by default I am a radiator too. Like attracts like. As the old saying goes, 'birds of a feather flock together'.

The *Think it – Say it – Do it* model will only work if you practice self-honesty. You can do this now. Take a look at your life and who you spend most of your time with. Do they truly help you develop and grow both personally and professionally? Look around you now.

When you're at work and a colleague gets a promotion, do your peers congratulate them authentically? Or do they put down their success? When a friend achieves, do your peers celebrate authentically? Or do they downplay their success by saying something like, 'They were just lucky.' Answering these questions will give you an idea of who you are flocking with.

Different powers

Powers of five can also be different in different areas of your life. I have three sets that are linked to mine: family, friends and business.

Family. 'Blood is thicker than water' is another old saying – and you can't choose your family. This is true but you can choose who in your family you spend most of your time with. I was once told by a friend that family are like friends; they need to earn the right to be in your life. I now choose the radiators in my family rather than the drains.

Friends. This is the easiest one to work out; as they say, 'You can count your true friends on one hand.' I know lots of people but only a few make it into my inner circle. These are my power of five. A true friendship has intimacy and for you to have intimacy there needs to be real trust. Why? Because intimacy actually means *'into me you see'*. Knowing this will help you to separate a true friend from an acquaintance.

Business. This power of five can change continuously if you are progressing. When you want to learn and grow, you have to create powers of five that support this. To grow you need to be around those who can teach you. If you want to be a manager, hang around with managers. If you want to be a business owner, hang around with business owners. If you want to be an author, guess what? Hang around with authors.

———————••●••———————

You meet your best friend Gary for a coffee and a catch up.

'How's it going?' he asks. 'It's going great mate. I really want to set up a business delivering inspirational talks, training and coaching.'

'Wow, I like that idea! I'm sure you will make it a success. What are you going to call it, your business?' Gary asks. 'Unlocking Potential,' you reply. Gary says 'That works; you certainly unlock potential.' You both laugh.

'So, what's stopping you?' he asks.

'Well, in truth I don't know anything about business. I have been to the PSA and know that I can deliver but setting up a business is a whole different experience. I've got a website and my business cards are printed but it feels like I've got all the gear and no idea.'

As you say this, you remember a friend – Phil, a tiler – telling you about business networking events. You tell Gary. 'Let's have a look online,' he says. Straight off, you type 'business networking events' into Google.

The page refreshes and, boom, 'The Portsmouth Business Expo' appears at the top of the page. And it's on tomorrow. Gary laughs. 'This is definitely meant to be – better book your ticket!'

-••●•••-

It's 8.30am and you're walking into your first networking event. You have a pocket full of business cards and a belly full of enthusiasm. And no idea what to expect.

As you walk through the door, you stop and stare at the room. It is huge, with so many people. You are overwhelmed and feel like a fish out of water. You take a deep breath and walk around the room, just getting a feel. You're not talking to anyone, just listening and looking around. You take a programme to see what's happening. 'Speed networking session' catches your eye. You smile, as your first thought was 'speed dating'. You quickly decide that this is where you need to be.

A man notices you walking over to grab a coffee before things start.

'You can sit here if you like,' he says. He introduces himself as Ian Skinner and tells you he owns The Diverse Cleaning Company, an industrial cleaning business. He's easy to talk to; a warm and friendly man.

'What do you do?' he asks and, enthusiastically, you tell him your story and what you want to do. He listens intently and at the end says, 'Brilliant. Have you been networking before?' When you explain this is your first time, Ian shares some top tips – he's a veteran networker. You exchange business cards and he shakes your hand firmly, wishing you well.

You watch Ian walk away. At that exact moment, you feel a shift. You realise this is where you are meant to be. You are no longer looking around the room nervously. You see it through new eyes and say to yourself, *This is my new school. Now it's time to find my teachers and create my new power of five*'.

You suddenly notice the time; speed networking starts in five minutes. You gulp the rest of your coffee and dash off to your next lesson.

9: Bringing it all together

#TISIDI

Congratulations, you made it! This tells me you have what it takes to create success within your life. Living your life using the *Think It – Say It – Do It* model will support you to achieve so much. You will, if you choose to practice this model, see changes in your life.

We've covered so much in this book. These final chapters are a summary, Top Tips and a conclusion. If you feel you are sliding, then these chapters will help you refocus, without the need to re-read the whole book.

This chapter is a summary you can revisit any time. We all know that in life we find a way that works and then, for whatever reason, it disappears. This happens to me too. If this happens to you and you feel life is getting tough, I would suggest you pause and consider if you have lost momentum. If you think you have, read this chapter and use the Top Tips to get back on track.

Own your f**k ups

The first part of the *Think It – Say It – Do It* model is that you have to own your f**k ups. It's only then that you can start to make changes.

In the first chapter I talked about my f**k ups. I did this so you could see that, whatever yours are, they are unlikely to be as bad as mine! Most people don't like to admit they are wrong or can't do something. The truth is that when we admit we were wrong or couldn't to do it, we are taking the first step to creating success. I embrace my f**k ups: they make me human. The difference with me now is I learn from mine, so I stop repeating them.

First, *Think it*

The model starts with *Think it*. This is a tough area as we are talking about our minds. We think constantly, so much it can be just one big noise. The mind is also the king of sabotage. It is always pooh-poohing your ideas. You think about something you want to do and straight away your mind tells you why you can't do it.

These thoughts can be influenced by your past. It is the interjects others have given you. Those well-meaning adults in your childhood, or friends and colleagues in the years since.

It is the 'You shouldn't do this; you shouldn't do that.' Or, even worse, 'You *can't* do this and you *can't* do that.'

Next, *Say it*

Now is the time to *Say it*. The only way to overcome these thoughts is to move onto the second section of the model, *Say it*.

Now is the time to:

say 'I am more than my thoughts'

get off the thought roundabout and do something different

create a change

Say it.

I do this every day through self-affirmations. I tell myself every day what I *can* and *will* do. Maybe now is the time for you to start telling yourself what it is you can and will do.

Choose your audience

Saying it is the most powerful part of the model. The only issue is who you *Say it* to. There are so many people out there with an opinion. These people can sometimes do more harm than good.

You will have people who are naysayers. They may have their own internal battles. These are not the people to *Say it* to.

Find those people around you who believe in you. Those people that want you to be the most successful you can be. They are there – you just need to seek them out. Get out a pen and paper. Now.

What family do you have? Friends? Colleagues? Acquaintances? List them all now. See who you can *Say it* to.

The people on your list are the next step to you creating success. They will be the ones who continuously encourage you to take the next step: *Do it*.

Then, *Do it!*

The final part is *Do it*, and *doing it* is never as easy as it sounds. (If it was, we wouldn't need books like this). So, what stops us? Can you remember?

It's fear…

Do you remember my story about the boy and the monster under his bed?

The boy created fear from the influences around him. We do this every day. Our peers, social media, TV, politicians; they all create irrational fears.

Revisit fear

Now let's look at fear again. Do you remember how I broke down fear? If not, here it is again:

False
Evidence
Appearing
Real

This false evidence is fed to us every day and our minds make it appear real. Now, how many times in your life have you overcome a fear?

Think back. Maybe it was learning to ride a bike, drive a car or swim in the sea. What did you get when you overcame that fear?

I'll tell you. What you got was *freedom*. And not only that, you changed the word 'fear' to this:

Factual
Evidence (that is)
Actually
Real

Embrace 'failure'

The final reason people don't *Do it* is they fear or avoid failure. This is a big mistake as failure is just a stepping stone to success.

66

Remember when I told you about James Dyson – who invented the Dyson bagless vacuum cleaner? He famously stated that he'd created 5,126 prototypes. Did he fail 5,126 times? Dyson's mindset saw it differently; he knew that every failure would eventually lead to his greatest success.

This brings us back to the quote I took from my good friend Mark Legg, who says FAIL means:

First
Attempt
In
Learning

(In James Dyson's case, it was the 5,126th attempt in learning!)

When failing, we have to link to those we *Say it* to. These are the people who will support you to continue and create the success you are looking for. No man, woman or child is an island. We all need the help of others. We always *Do it* best when we have people who will champion us from the stands.

The true definition of failure, in my view, is not to try at all.

So, now we have reconnected with the *Think it – Say it – Do it* model.

Driving lessons to success

We now need to remind ourselves about the nuts and bolts: the driving lessons. First, build the vehicle that will transport you to the success you desire. The number one ingredient? A support network. This is not always straightforward.

If you are doing something new, you will have to put in some effort to create a support network that is linked to that area. Research and find the people who can help you. When you find this group, you will probably be the most unintelligent person in the room. This is a good thing as you will be ready and open to learn.

Remember, these people have trodden the path you are now walking. These people will know the pitfalls that await you. With their support and guidance, you can avoid the pain of falling into them.

When in the groups you will need to develop relationships with new people. Though some people find this easier than others, it is never easy.

I have a tip: ask questions. Most people like to talk about themselves. Just introduce yourself and ask, 'So, what do you do?' They will love this and tell you all about themselves. If you need more information, follow up with 'So, how did you get into doing that?'

Their answers will let you know if they can help you or not. My relationship process will help you separate the wheat from the chaff:

rapport – early conversational exchanges, the getting-to-know-you process

test and deliver – you ask for advice or a suggestion

trust – the person consistently delivers and meets your needs.

Remember, support networks come and go. They change as you do. If you feel you are giving more than getting in your network, it may be time to look for a new one. Sometimes you will become the most intelligent person in the room — always the teacher and never the pupil. We need to be both: this is how we learn, grow and develop.

Fill-up with fuel

Driving lesson two is about what fuels the car. We need that internal drive, however much support we get from others.

The top five personal attributes that fuel success are:

self-awareness

emotional intelligence

honesty

being open-minded

having unshakeable self-belief.

With this fuel you will have a vehicle that will go the distance. Trust me, I know. If you ignore or substitute these, you could end up breaking down in the desert of despair. Look for books — print or audio — or podcasts that cover these areas. Build your knowledge and self-confidence. Is this easy? No. So, gain strength and help yourself with the 30-day self-affirmation practice.

Self-affirmation

Every morning for the next 30 days, I want you to look in the mirror. I want you to look at yourself.

I want you to look deep into your own eyes. I want you to tell yourself:

I believe in you.

You can be anything you want to be.

Today I will... then set a goal linked to your long-term vision.

Practice this discipline for 30 days and see how your belief in yourself grows.

The power of five

The final part to remember about creating a support network is the power of five. You represent the five people you most associate with. There are lots of sayings. 'Birds of a feather flock together' or 'Your network is your net worth'. That's true. Your net worth is not just money; it's knowledge, emotion, friendship and so much more.

I learnt that if I wanted to be something new, I needed to find a new power of five. These come and go and have changed over time. Before starting out on my business journey, I didn't know many business owners. Today, my network is filled with business owners. Before I wrote my first book, I didn't know many authors. Today, my network is filled with authors.

Powers of five can be linked to many areas. Family, friends, fitness, education, business; the list goes on and on. You decide who will be in your power of five. Don't give these spaces away lightly. These people are the fuel that will bring you success.

Drains and radiators

I hope you remember drains and radiators. Avoid having drains in your power of five. Sometimes they still slip in and when they do, you need to act quickly or they will literally drain you. (My tip? *Run away!*)

Drains are easy to recognise. They are always moaning, They pooh-pooh your ideas. They don't deliver on their promises and they may even bad mouth you behind your back.

Radiators are the opposite. They always see the positives. They suggest new ideas. They help as and when you need it and they are selfless.

Get five of these and you will be very rich. Success will be at your fingertips.

Think back

So, we are at the end of the summary section and I want to end it simply. I told you about a quote I heard when coming to the end of my f**k up. These words are as important to me now as they were then:

'What we see we learn
What we learn we practice
What we practice we become
But what we become is not always who we are meant to be'

When you think about the f**k ups in your life, remember these words. Think about how you created your f**k ups:

what was the influence?

where did the behaviour come from?

how long have you practised these behaviours?

71

That's when you can say 'no more' and use the *Think it — Say it — Do it* model to bring you the success you deserve.

10: Top tips

#TISIDI

Top Tip #1 – Build a self-reflection routine

Reflection is a way for you to see if you are back on the roundabout.

Look at where you have come from. Was it where you wanted to be? Look into the future. Where are you going?

So many people in the world don't create time to reflect. People will always say that they have no time. I say this is rubbish. I was this person; I was a busy fool who never created a space to reflect. One day I was exhausted, with my head in my hands, thinking, *'I can't keep going on like this.'*

Though I felt like I wanted to just crawl into a hole and hide, I decided I had to find more time, somehow. Help came from my friend Mark. He had a routine where he got up early and used the 'extra' time to reflect, plan, meditate and exercise. Mark suggested that I make time to practice this too.

My first thought was how tired I'd be if I got up an hour earlier. Then I laughed. There it was, the head telling me why I couldn't. I thought about my evenings. I realised that, in truth, I could go to bed a little earlier and so could have the same amount of sleep. I now practice this regularly. Every morning I reflect, plan, meditate and exercise. My life is the best it's ever been.

Top Tip #2 – Refresh your network

Has your circle started to stagnate? Do you automatically know what people will say? You know when this is happening. It's on those days when you are looking for some company or inspiration. You start to look through your phone and contacts. No one jumps out at you. It's that thought that says 'same old, same old'.

This is when you need to take some action. If you are in business, this is the time to get out and network. At networking events, don't just go up to those you know. Make a decision to speak to new faces. Also, commit yourself to set up at least two 1-2-1 meetings after the event. This is a simple and effective way to increase your network and find new opportunities and possibilities.

Do you find that all your friends and colleagues spout the same old opinions and have the same interests? Maybe it's time to create new friends. I bet your head says '*how do I do that?*' Well, it's easy if you are willing to put in some action and *Do it.*

When you're at work don't just talk to the people you always talk to. Approach those you don't know. Who knows where it could lead?

Maybe you could look at a new hobby? Dancing, cooking, amateur dramatics, yoga… the list goes on. You could meet so many new people with new thoughts or new ideas.

Most people use Facebook or social media like it. We all have friends who have friends that we don't know. Send them a personal message, strike up a conversation. You have no idea what hidden gems are within your network.

Top Tip #3 – Take action, often

Action is key. I was once told 'if nothing changes, nothing changes'. This is so true. And change only comes through action.

You can have the best network in the world. They can have ideas that flow all day long. They can give you the best tips and suggestions. But in truth, without you putting in the action, they are just words floating in the wind.

It is only *you* who can plant these words into the ground. The planting is the action. It is doing what needs to be done. It is going against your fear, doubt and disbelief. It is being comfortable with being uncomfortable. Every action causes a reaction. Whatever you do, there is always an outcome. It is these outcomes that lead onto your next action.

If you feel that you are not getting where you want to be then this is down to you. You can make up every excuse in the world but the buck stops with you. Inaction is your choice and action is your choice too. I was once told 'don't see a wall as a block, look at it as an obstacle'.

There is no wall you can't get over, through, around or under. You get past obstacles with planning and action.

Don't look at action as something that needs to be huge. Imagine a plant with healthy foliage, full of colour and life. This plant will bring joy to everyone who sees it. Plants also support the whole environment. They release oxygen into the atmosphere, absorb carbon dioxide.

How did this plant get to a place where it breeds success? Simple, it was through your small actions; daily checks on feed and water, a weekly prune and quarterly pot change. Your actions need only be simple and, in time, they will

75

benefit you and the world around you.

Top Tip #4 – Grow your knowledge

I was once told that 'knowledge is power'. In truth, I did not know what they meant. Over time, I have started to think more about this saying. In the early days, I believed that having knowledge meant I would have power over others. I know today that this is not true. I also don't need to be more powerful than anyone else.

Today, I believe that knowledge *gives* you the power to have control over your future. You have the power to decide who you want to be. It also gives you the power to make informed choices, as knowledge lets you see the bigger picture. Knowledge is all around us. You reading this now is giving you more knowledge. We are in a world now where information is at our fingertips.

If you are reading this and you don't have a smart phone, tablet or computer then I will eat my hat. Though these technological devices offer knowledge in abundance, many of you will not even have scratched the surface of what you could learn. That's because we have distractions that get in the way of us absorbing knowledge.

Don't sit there watching brain-dead TV. Don't sit there scrolling through social media and getting caught up in other people's dramas. Instead, use social media to follow great leaders, spiritual speakers or successful business owners. You can connect with their podcasts and YouTube channels and absorb all their content.

Books are the true food of the gods. I used to be one of those people who had 'no time to read'. Though time was an issue, I also knew I found it difficult to sit quietly and read. My mind is always going from one thought to another and another and another… Ideas come thick and fast. I shared this challenge with a friend and they told me about an audio book app. I checked it out and, my god, my life changed.

It was one of those small actions that was like planting an acorn. That acorn grew into a mighty oak and today I have audio books on the go all the time. I listen to these at every opportunity. Now I'm building knowledge when I'm driving, running, cycling, in the gym and doing housework.

Top Tip #5 – Drop the drains, embrace the radiators

This is the quickest and easiest to say. Positivity – having a glass-half-full – is your key to success.

Don't listen to the haters, doubters and disbelievers. Avoid toxicity. If something's going to drag you down, step away from it right now. This also means the media. What benefit do we actually get from watching the news and reading tabloids? It's all doom and gloom and breeds fear (False Evidence Appearing Real). This takes up unwanted space and gets in the way of your creativity.

Some of the doubters, haters and disbelievers may be people you have known for many years. They may be people you love and care for deeply. I am not saying walk away from them literally. You could be the one to help them; you could shift their mindset. You could be the hand that pulls them onto the life raft of peace and success.

If they are not ready to change, that's ok. Just meet them and chew the fat and don't get drawn in. I have friends like this. I don't tell them all that I do or all I believe. It is pointless: they don't understand and are content with what they know.

If I tried to force my opinions onto them, I am at risk. I could easily be pulled out of the life raft and back into the turbulent sea of what once was.

Remember, the world is full of *drains* and *radiators*. You are a radiator and you need to be around other radiators. They are easily seen. Make a beeline for them, connect with them either face to face or via technology. Watch what they do, ask them questions and then follow their lead. A true leader (radiator) creates other leaders. When you follow this path, people will see what you are doing. It is then that they start to follow you and mirror how you developed your success. Helping yourself will undoubtedly end up helping others.

We have to be selfish to be selfless… and that is a whole new book.

11: Conclusion

#TISIDI

This book was written during the COVID-19 pandemic in 2020. It was a tough time for most people. You could sense the global feelings of loss and confusion. Nobody truly had any idea of what the new 'normal' would look like. I decided to use the time to write this book and share the *Think it – Say it – Do it* model with the world.

I had the thought and straightaway I said, 'Yes, I can do that.' Then I shared the idea with my power of five (*Say it*). They said go for it and gave some useful tips and ideas. I then created a plan of how I was going to get it done.

I'd like to say it all happened exactly as planned. If I did, I'd be lying.

I hit the floor running and completed over 14,000 words in 10 days. The *Do it* part of the model was in action every day. I was on track to have the whole book written within a month. If that was the case, then why am I sat here, seven months later, finally finishing the book?

Well, I'll tell you: I got side-tracked. I had more *Think it – Say it – Do it* moments. This meant that rather than having just one project, I had around five. Because I'd created more than I could manage, I put the book further and further down the list.

You may be wondering why I'm telling you this. Well,

that's easy, I want you to use this model, so it works. I don't want you to end up in the place I've just been. I once heard a saying, 'It's better to do one or two things really well than many things badly'. That is so true.

That's what happened to me. I f**ked up by trying to take on too much. Eventually, I did pull it together and that's why you are reading this now.

If you want this model to work, try it in just one area first. It could be losing weight, getting fit, writing a book, climbing a mountain, learning to sail a boat.

Whatever it is, just choose one thing to concentrate on. Do this a few times in different areas that you want to change so that you see the benefit. Once you have this embedded, you can start to use it time and again.

I have learnt so much about my own programme over the past few months. I have learnt now that I can do multiple *Think it – Say it – Do it* tasks at the same time but it takes a whole new set of disciplines.

Hey, maybe that could be the sequel to this book… there you go, I'm at it again!

Acknowledgements

We are only the people we are today because of the people who have helped us on our journey. I want to acknowledge some of those and others that may not have been among those mentioned within this book.

Firstly, I would like to say a really big thank you to my family. They have all stayed by my side during this journey and have continued to support all of my decisions, no matter where they have led. Thank you in no particular order Adele Hodge, Jordan Hodge, Karen Stewart, Henry Stewart, Tilly Stewart, Sadie Jones, Alfie Clarke, Lacy Jones, Louise Clarke and my Mum. I would also like to say another thank you to my other Mummy, Lesley Hodge, and Daddy, Dave Hodge – two beautiful people that have always shown me love and care.

I have another family too and this is my beautiful partner Ruth Ancell, who is a gift that I treasure and who will soon be my wife. I also have my best friend Gary Clark Allan and his partner Stacy Clark Allan and beautiful son Jaden. Gary is so much more than a friend and I have the most amount of love for the support he always gives.

I also want to thank the many professionals who supported my journey of change. It was these people who helped me to take personal responsibility and supported me to be the person I am today.

I would like to personally thank Jo Purdy, Allan Rodden,

Debbie Willis, Jo Bushell, Hilary Stanton and then many others who never gave up on me. I am also happy to say that these wonderful people are still in my life today and they encourage me as much now as they did then.

I have gone from having no work history in 2006 to becoming a successful business owner. Apparently, I do have to take some credit for this (so I'm told). I do acknowledge my part, but I am in no doubt that the main reason for this is because of the opportunities I was given. I would like to thank all those people that got me started on my journey. These are Tony Weeks, Stuart McDowell, Cecile Todd, Sandra Hanson, Bruce Marr, Kelly Anderson.

Every single one of these amazing people developed me professionally. It was these amazing people that took me from being a volunteer to a service manager overseeing a staff team of 40. These amazing people could see my potential and pushed me to think, say and do more.

I have a final and special thank you, and this is to Mark Legg, who is the author of *Business Builder: Plan, Develop & Build a "7" Figure Trade Business*. I met Mark on my entrepreneurial journey and this man has taught me so much and has helped me tap into a whole new level of potential. I am so grateful for the knowledge and support this man has given me.

About the author

Gethin is not your typical behaviour change specialist.

He hasn't got an academic pedigree: what he has got is experience. Gethin excels at the job because he has made dramatic, lasting changes to his own behaviour that have taken him from a prison cell to the boardroom.

He's been there and done that (usually getting caught in the process!).

Gethin grew up in care, spent eight years in prison and was an intravenous drug user for many years. He was on a clear path towards repeated prison sentences and an early death.

His transformation began in 2000, when he decided to stop running from himself. He started a six-year therapeutic journey that included psychotherapy, acceptance and commitment therapy (ACT) and cognitive behavioural therapy (CBT).

His lived experience developed in tandem with his psychological journey: as his self-love and self-knowledge grew, he moved through detox, volunteering and paid work, until he became the behaviour change specialist he is today.

Gethin now supports leadership teams and coaches who want to implement personal and corporate change.

He's recognised for his strong leadership and influencing skills. Energetic and enthusiastic, he balances honesty with compassion.

As a powerful, entertaining and inspiring professional speaker, Gethin challenges individuals and teams to recognise their potential, while being aware of their mind-traps. For Gethin, it's about helping his audience take personal responsibility for making change.

Gethin has a unique combination of academic, professional and personal experience. This means he can 'pick and mix' an approach that matches the needs of an organisation, team or individual seeking change for the better.

After all, change for the better isn't an academic exercise for Gethin, it's his purpose and his mission.

You can contact Gethin directly through his website www.unlockingthepotential.co.uk or you can follow Gethin on Twitter @GethinUnlocks, LinkedIn or on Facebook Gethin Jones Unlocking Potential.

Printed in Great Britain
by Amazon

82671890R00058